Beyond Rainbows

By Kevin Ross Emery

No matter how hard we would like to make things, people, places or events in our life black & white, they are all truly filled with the colors of the rainbow.

Tears, fears, rainy days, and times of endless sunshine have helped create the colors of this rainbow.

I dedicate this to all my lovers: male, female, and in-between, I bless my life...it has never been boring.

3 March 2007

Table of Contents

Safe Sex	6
Would You Laugh	7
Lover of Women	8
Split Apart	10
You and I	11
Broken Promises	13
Mathematically	14
Still Special	15
Yours No More	16
But Physically	17
Mexican Stand Off	18
Sweat	19
Clearly	20
Mine to Keep	21
Tell Me Why	22
Condemn	23
My Garden	24
The Patron	25
These Are the Nights	26
Nightmares & Dreams	27
Tigers	29
Early Morning Loving	30
Turning Away	31
Betrayed	32
Not Broken	33
A Gay Man's Epitaph	35
Fair Exchange	36
Not Failure	37
Twin Bears	39
A Memoriam to the Last Great War	40
Hidden	42
Odd Times	45
Unspoken Thoughts to My Lover	46
A War Cry	47
If I Had	49
Once More	50

Vampire	51
In Being	52
Aids Scare	53
One Last Time	54
Voyeur	55
Alone	56
In Need	58
Peaches	59
When Friends Become Lovers	60
And the Pedestal Cracks	61
Just Friends	62
Rainbows & Tears	63
Why You Run	64
And the Season Turns	65
Looking for Rainbows	66

Safe Sex

We have made the sex,
      As safe,
As the sex can be.
      There are no guarantees.

It is not the sex,
      That worries me,
It is the making love,
      That I fear,
For there are no guarantees there either.

1987

Would You Laugh?

Would you laugh,
    If you knew my inner thoughts,
And knew,
    How afraid I am that you will leave.

Could you understand,
    About all the others,
Who have left me before?

Do you know,
    How much your reassuring hugs,
And words of love,
    Mean to me?

Is it possible,
    For you to tell me,
That you love me,
    Just a little more often than you do,
Or would you laugh.

Lover of Women

You are a straight man,
        Happily heterosexual
A lover of women
        I have met a million of you.

I see what you love
        When I look into your eyes
You like the chase
        The capture, the conquest.

You do not love women,
        How can you?
When you do not even love
        Yourself.

Love women?
        You, who disdain and disrespect
Denigrate and dismiss them
        Love women?

I think not
        All I see is hate
Condescension and fear,
        Great.

And yet I see you grin
        Laugh and smile and love
Give and be giving
        As long as it's with one of the boys
Or sometimes the dog
        But only sometimes.

Do us all a favor
        Will you
Now don't squirm
        Just donate the sperm.

Pay a prostitute
 So at least she gets
Something
 Out of it

And then go study
 with a gay man
for he will teach you
 how to love women.

Split Apart

In days of yore,
        And times of old,
When the earth was new,
        And I knew you.

We were a part of one,
        My split apart,
And when separated we were,
        You took with you half my heart.

As a child leaves the womb,
        A part of its mother it shall always be,
Just as we became our won whole,
        As we both evolved after you split apart from me.

But I can never truly be,
        All that is meant of me,
Without the other half of my heart,
        That you took away when we split apart, my split apart.

You and I

Here we are, you and I,
      You, a boy,
Starting to become a man,
      And I a man,
Who was not long enough a boy.

I see dreams in your eyes,
      And can tell the sincerity,
Of your innocence,
      I can appreciate it

It makes me melancholy,
      To think of all I lost,
Along the way,
      Growing up too fast.

I can but try,
      To help you,
Lose,
      Your innocence.

It is not,
      Of jealousy,
That I want you to lose it,
      But because of gentleness.

Because I know,
      I can help you gently lose your innocence,
Appreciate being a man,
      As you have appreciated being a boy.

You are to the time now,
      Where I see,
Innocence has just started to slip away,
      And it can be such a painful parting.

That is why,

        I would like to make it
As gentle
        As possible

Come, trust me,
        I would not hurt you,
Intentionally,
        No never would I hurt you intentionally.

I just want to share,
        What I know,
Try to show you what I've seen,
        Warn you of what I now know of.

This is what,
        I can do for you,
If you let me,
        If you want me to.

And I do it.
        For the most selfish of reasons,
For as you lost your innocence,
        I shall, if for only a moment, be recapturing part of mine.

Broken Promises

I wait for a call,
    That never comes,
Hurting from the sting
    Of another broken promise.

Not only have you broken your promises,
    But you have allowed me to make up your excuses.
For I was thinking it was to hide them from my friends,
    When it was actually hiding them from me.

I was taught to cry when something dies,
    But through your broken promises I can see I was nothing.
So I shall have nothing to cry about
    As I stop listening for the phone to ring
And start again to live in a world
    With no more broken promises.

Mathematically

We charge forward,
    Into each other,
Hurting each other,
    Upon impact.

Traveling,
    Intertwined once,
Now we pull apart,
    Each direction on the other side of the other.

We pass through each other,
    In unspoken anger,
Tearing, silently, through the fabric,
    Of our mutual interdependent existence.

Though unraveling,
    It is still joined,
It still tears,
    It still hurts.

We hold on,
    In little ways,
We let go,
    In larger ones.

Mathematically,
    I know,
All too soon the feelings will be negative,
    And still we hold on.

Still Special

Years have passed,
    Affections have changed,
As we have,
    Lovers once, friends forever.

In a time of need,
    When you needed to be needed,
I was there to hold you,
    Know I will be there always.

Within our embrace,
    Vivid memories of our moments – of passion?
Entered my mind,
    And left me with warm feelings.

You,
    You'll never know,
How much it meant to me,
    That you let me be there for you,
Especially with all that has passed between us.

It still feels good to hold you,
    And to be held by you.
After all these years,
    It's so special,
Let's keep it that way, always.

Yours No More

Tell me why,
    I should give you my rights,
Let you control my days,
    And judge my nights?

What is left,
    Of the Land of the free,
If I allowed you to choose my God,
    Lower my head and bend my knee?

And if I cower,
    In the home of the brave,
And can't say what I think,
    Then is there anything left to save?

For two hundred years,
    Or more,
You asked for the gift of the tired, hungry and poor,
    Building this nation's wealth upon,
The back of the huddled masses,
    But what if I wish to huddle no more?

You kill in the name,
    Of a flag
That use to be mine.

You persecute in the name
    Of a flag,
That use to be mine.

You judge and punish me,
    In the name of a flag,
That use to be mine.

Who gave my flag to you?
    I take back my flag,
For the land of the free and the home of the brave,
    Because your bigotry makes you neither.

18 October 2007

But Physically

If you cannot touch me,
    But physically,
Then do not touch me,
    At all.

Though my body,
    May respond.
My mind will hate you,
    For leaving it behind.

1981

Mexican Stand-Off

So much,
    Is passing between us,
All of it unsaid,
    It is a Mexican stand-off.

I know,
    You care,
You know,
    I care.

You refer to a future,
    I withdraw,
I refer to a future,
    You withdraw.

I give,
    You take.
You give,
    I take.

Still it is a Mexican stand-off

How soon,
    Before one of us,
Will admit,
    We are falling in love.

You say,
    You're scared,
I say,
    I am sacred,
Neither say why.

How long will it be...
    A Mexican stand-off.
1987

Sweat

It is the sweat
        I most like to lick
The salty, free flowing
        Sweat
That washes your body

Your body in need
        In need of my touch
Your body yearning
        For release

You arch,
        My tongue reaches
Fingers entwined
        In a grasp tighter
Than a wrestlers grasp

You cannot find release
        Until I release you
Release, we release
        And the dawn breaks
And the bed breaks
        Sweat.

Clearly

Tell me
        What you're telling me
Make sure I know
        What you've told me.

You may say it so clearly
        In your ears
But has it reached
        My ears, jumbled.

Let me know
        If you are going
I do not want to look for you.
        To find you've gone.

Mine to Keep

I give to you my heart,
        But I warm you,
It is like a boom-a-rang,
        No matter how much I send it out,
It comes back, stronger than ever.

It does not mean,
        That you may not keep my love,
With which it was sent,
        But you cannot have my heart,
For it is mine to keep,
        You see there are others,
With whom I share it.

1982

Tell Me Why?

When did you stop loving me
        Like you did before?
How did I miss the change
        Or were my eyes closed?

Trust and Honesty
        Were your key words
When it began
        Even omission, was a lie

Now I know you lied to me
        Instead of telling me why
You did not want to be with me
        Was it so much easier?

I'm not sure your answers
        Will not hurt
But I hurt already
        So tell me why?

1984

Condemn

It is easier to condemn in ignorance,
    Than to risk conflict,
It is easier to listen to someone else version of the world,
    Then to go to the source and have your reality challenged.

It is easier to hurt someone from a distance-
    Passively.
Than to stand close and have to observe their
    Pain.

How hard it is...
    To be the bad guy.
Who no one tells them why they are the bad guy.
    But just treat them that way.

As the immortal bard once said...
    "If you cut me,
Do I not bleed?"
    Red are my tears.

2003

My Garden

Hummingbirds, butterflies and bees,
    All flying free,
Paying homage to the splendor,
    Of the Bee Balm, in my garden.

Unaware of their beauty,
    Or symmetry,
They just be,
    My hummingbird, butterflies and bees.

Oh, they scourge my gardens
    Completely,
And may flirt with a lily,
    Or black-eyed Susan or Pansy.

But as they all fly free,
    They pay respect to her majesty,
The Bee Balm
    Which rules my garden.

The Patron

I was happy with what I had,
    For I had you, for today.
Then you filled me with such grand dreams,
    Of tomorrow and forever.

You talked constantly of us,
    And painted such pictures
To make the most in love couple,
    Envious of what we had, even though we had nothing.

Oh you were a painter, a poet and a dreamer,
    And I thought I was your inspiration.
But I see now I was but your patron;
    Supporting you in your finer arts of dreaming.

You now have a new patron,
    One who thinks they are your inspiration.
And what have I?
    I have left the memories,
Of what was to be,
    Along with several empty dreams.

These Are the Nights

And these are the nights,
    I miss you most.
Coming home, to a house,
    Makes me not want to come home at all.

It was not that it was such a bad night,
    But it really was not good.
And when the good was really hard to see,
    You always managed to find it for me.

I know it is really too late to call,
    Besides you have your life now,
Just as I have mine,
    And it is just one of those nights, I will survive.

But these are the nights,
    I miss you most,
And talking to my stuffed animals will have to do,
    I just wish they could hold me when I start to cry.

Nightmares & Dreams

I spoke of my dreams,
    You heard them as your nightmares,
So as I embellished on them,
    You silently hated them.

You never told me of all the unpleasant emotions,
    My words unleashed in you,
You so wanted to keep me,
    You just ignored my dreams.

You did not share,
    How you had heard,
Those dreams before,
    How you shared them before.

You did not tell me,
    How they had turned into nightmares,
Of all the pain,
    They had caused you.

Then again,
    I did not ask,
I did not ask if you wanted to share,
    My dreams.

I just made them,
    Our dreams,
Never asked, took your silence,
    As agreement.

You followed,
    Slowly being driven,
Further and further,
    - away.

By the time you spoke,
    You were so far away,

I could barely hear or understand,
        What you were saying.

I could have used different words,
        We could,
Perhaps,
        have found mutual ones.

But we no longer talk,
        To each other,
But we now speak,
        At each other.

The dreams,
        Are shattered,
Only the nightmares,
        -survived.

Tigers

Tigers tangled,
    Curled like cubs,
        Washing away the dirt.
            Of a thousand years.

Entwined
    Enmeshed,
        Embolden,
           Embodied.

Endless love,
    Infinite caring,
        Two cubs,
           Two tigers,
                Serving the same Master.

2002

Early Morning Love

Half asleep,
    I reach for the warmth of your body,
Half aroused,
    You snuggle up to me.

One moment,
    We are wrestling like children,
The next,
    Like lovers.

Covers become construed,
    Early morning nips at us,
And we huddle together,
    Hiding in the warmth of each other's body.

Half asleep,
    Half aroused.
A little playful,
    A little playfully.

Then asleep again,
    Peacefully like children,
And yet,
    More so like lovers.

1981

Turning Away

You have grown comfortable with me,
    Allowing me to see all those sides of you,
No one else ever sees,
    I treasure that.

You have let me into your home,
    Shared your fears,
And your faults,
    That make you so special.

Those things you hide from the world,
    Afraid they will judge you,
Condemn you.
    These are the things I find most endearing.

You've held me, I've cried,
    Comforted me when I was sick,
And been there,
    When I was hurt.

It is no wonder I love you so much.

It is only when you turned away,
    That it hurt so much,
Please don't turn away
    -anymore.

The kind of love we share,
    I know I can count on forever,
It is one of those loves that grows strong,
    And will never hurt again.

Please don't turn away, please.

Betrayed

In shadowy recesses,
        Hidden away,
Behind intentionally locked doors,
        Lies the truth.

Well protected,
        Behind the layers;
Layers of excuses,
        Layers of denial.

The doorways are protected by the fears,
        The fears of the hurt, the pain, and the emptiness,
A fear that nothing would be left,
        But tears who would never stop.

Am I ready to release the needs?
        I needed you to be my knight in shining armor,
I needed you to be different than the others.
        And yet wasn't it you, who let the child be abused, dirtied and used.

There are more kinds of abusers,
        Than the ones who raise their hands, their voices,
Even dropped their pants,
        Maybe that is why I couldn't see you for your abuses.

No, you did not bruise the body,
        Nor did you penetrate the child,
You didn't even hurl the verbal hate,
        But you sold the child out, did you not?

Was not my body, my mind and my soul,
        Traded for your dreams, or was it your denial?
So now your armor has gotten rusty,
        And fallen off.

Where do I go from here?

Not Broken

I am not broken,
    Do not try & fix me,
I am changing; I am facing a thousand pains,
    Hitherto unfaced, but I am not broken.

I also am not,
    Who you knew,
When this whole thing began,
    I am in the process of becoming whole again,
Or perhaps for the very first time.

But as I bring in the pieces,
    The edges may be sharp,
And I do not mean to hurt you,
    But try not to hold onto what I need to let go of.

And as I wander,
    In and out of my little cave,
Let me know that you are out there for me,
    But do not force your way in,
Or try to force me out.

Because I do not openly weep,
    Do not think I do not weep.
And when I speak of my pain, if it is not in agony,
    Do not question the validity of it,
Perhaps the pain is agony enough for me.

Do not invalidate it because it is spoken in quiet tones,
    One does not need,
To wail or be hysterical,
    To be in pain.

Also do not try to take from me,
        My understanding that this all does happen,
For larger reasons,
        It may sound like excuses to you,
But it is my light at the end of my tunnel.

13 March 2003

A Gay Man's Epitaph

When they put me in the ground,
    And erect a slab of marble at my head,
It will not talk of vices,
    As the reason that I am dead.

More likely it will say,
    Cause of death: others,
Family who cared, friends who nagged,
    And inconsiderate lovers.

1980's

Fair Exchange

Thoughts jumbled,
      You've given me love,
Comfort and support,
      But trust?

In your times of need,
      You need no one,
But yourself,
      And I am left on the other side.

When you even think I am in need you come,
      Caring & giving, hurt if I do not share,
So how am I to feel,
      When I am not allowed to share?

You take such delight in doing for me,
      Why can't you realize I love you as you love me,
So allow me the pleasures,
      I allow you.

Not Failure

As another relationship closes,
    I become the object of pity.
Will I ever get it right?
    They wonder.

I wasn't aware,
    That I had gotten it wrong.
Do they know that?
    I wonder.

As each relationship closes,
    I take inventory of what,
I have gained,
    Insights, memories, new friends, new awareness,

Also I look at what other things I acquired,
    Tough lessons,
Times of red eyes,
    And unpleasant feelings.

But for me,
    The bottom line has always been,
And will always be,
    Did I grow or did I just re-create?

And if I did just re-create,
    Then it is time for me to learn.
To break the pattern,
    But if it was a chance of growth.

And if I did,
    If I learned,
And I became more,
    Then I succeeded.

Succeed more than those who participate,
        In ongoing stagnation,
To please their peers,
        Rather than risking being seen as a failure.

But neither starting,
        Nor ending,
A relationship, for growth
        Is failing.

So it was not
        failure,
It was not a
        mistake,
I am not wrong,
        again.

Twin Bears

Twin bears,
        I bear
& me bear,
        To look at them you cannot tell the difference.

But I can see the difference,
        Between what I bear wants,
And what you want,
        Of me bear.

But they are both the same bear- in a way,
        For I bear
& me bear.
        Both just want to be loved.

A Memoriam to the Last Great War
(War on Aids)

I look into the eyes,
> Of the victims of the last great war.

Eyes of pain,
> Waiting for peace.

War that kills,
> The old,

And robs the young,
> Sentencing them to death in the womb.

The last great war,
> Has no winners,

Except perhaps for the few who claim victory,
> In the deaths of those who are not like themselves.

Fueling fear,
> With accusation,

That this is the war of vengeance,
> Being waged by a wrathful and angry God.

By those who will march,
> And kill for the right to live,

As long as they can choose those,
> That they feel should have that right.

Do they know their God,
> Is our God?

Can love even those,
> Filled with darkness and hatred.

But on some level,
> I know that they do,

So they continue knowing,
> That god will even love them.

But this is a memoriam,

To the last great war,
To the millions who have,
    And shall die.

One whose deadly destructiveness,
    Is fueled,
By hatred and ignorance,
    By fear and hypocrisy.

I look into the eyes of its victims,
    Who are pleading for one more day.
And yet for a painless tomorrow.
    Know they cannot have both.

Before you pontificate,
    And justify,
Your unwillingness to commit
    To ending of the best great war.

Remember victims are not only,
    Those who die.
But those who,
    Are left behind.

And with that I ask you to look,
    At the next victims,
Of the last great war,
    You will find them in the mirror.

Hidden

You ask why do I not stay,
        Just hidden.
It is okay to be me,
        As long as I do not tell you about it.

You are sure I am all right,
        In some perverse way,
So if I just don't tell you,
        Then you can like me in your ignorance.

Speak not,
        Of the things you know not,
Except through the front pages,
        Of the supermarket counter magazines.

And you are to Christian,
        To want to see me bleed,
You gave that sport up a hundred years ago.
        But you also do not want to hear about my pain.

And do not let you know, that I can be human,
        And be one of them,
For they are animals,
        And you know me.

For I am your friend,
        That held you when you were in pain,
When all the others turned their back,
        Uncomfortable with your grief.

Perhaps I am your brother or sister,
        The aunt or uncle to your children,
Someone you use to fight with, dream with,
        Maybe you even took baths with me.

I might be a favorite cousin,
        Or a treasured school teacher.

The person who at some point has changed your life,
    In a positive way.

I am your father or mother,
    I am your child and your friend,
And it okay,
    As long as I am hidden.

As long as I perpetuate your fairy tales,
    Discreetly avoid certain conversations,
Or better yet even lie.
    It makes you feel better.

It's okay as long as I am hidden,
    Shoved away in dark corners,
Left in dark alley's and am not the one,
    That got beaten to death while walking home.

It's okay,
    As long as you don't see or hear my pain,
And can hide in your ignorance,
    Telling yourself your lies, asking me to confirm them.

Yes, it is better,
    Better for you,
For if you come out of hiding,
    You might have to grow.

Growth is painful,
    And pain that is mine is easy for you,
Easier than to risk,
    The pain you might feel if you grow.

For in that growth,
    You might realize,
That you are not,
    God's only child.

And sometimes,

Those people in black robes,
That spew hate in the name of God,
    Might have lied to you.

And if they lied to you about that,
    What else did they lie to you about,
Perhaps they do not know,
    The way to Heaven.

What if you cannot just sit back,
    In stagnation,
And go to heaven?
    Maybe you might have to go through the pain of becoming human.

No, it is better,
    If it is hidden,
Do not work to hard to become human,
    Do not upset all you've been told, of course THEY are right.

But as you drift,
    Off to sleep, tonight,
If you question THEM,
    Keep it hidden.

Do not show your doubts,
    Feel no pain, for anyone but yourself,
And fall asleep dreaming of HOW you will get your wings,
    -not if.

Odd Times

I think of you,
      At odd times,
And when I think of you,
      They are odd thoughts.

I find myself,
      One moment, smiling,
The next laughing,
      Then serious again.

Excited,
      I want to talk to you.
Disturbed,
      I want to talk to you.

Then I realize,
      I just want,
To talk to you,
      To be with you.

When will I see you again?
      I wonder,
But do not worry,
      For I know I shall.

And I am in no hurry,
      To push you,
Or be pushed by you.
      At this moment,
I just want to be with you.

1986

Unspoken Thoughts to My Lover

You have gone to find yourself,
    And it is time,
I go and find myself,
    But so much left unsaid.

Perhaps if I could have spoken,
    All the fears and dreams I had,
And you could have spoken yours,
    We would not be parting now.

I know you did not understand,
    All I did and said,
Nor did I of you,
    But it is behind us now,

And yet I can't help but think,
    Of all we lost along the way,
And all we are losing now because of;
    The Unspoken Thoughts to My Lover.

A War Cry

I am done here,
>My work at this place comes to an end.

And though I will be back,
>It will not be the same.

This place has brought me much,
>And I leave it with great sadness

Even as I am called to new places,
>And know much awaits there for me.

I surrender what is familiar,
>I surrender what is comfortable,

I take what Master gives me for the next part of my journey,
>And I enter off into war.

For make no mistake,
>It is war,

Make no mistake,
>I will win, for to lose is not an option.

But not gone-yet.
>I grieve for what falls away.

For I shall miss this place.
>And who I was when I was here.

And I shall miss,
>My relationships that were here with me,

For even those that survive,
>Will not be the same.

Master has given me,
>For my journey,

One to cover my back, keep me strong and love me unconditionally
>I can ask for nothing more.

But there is no,
>You and me against the world, here,

I have done that,

>And no longer need to be there.

For this time,
>It is a you
And a me,
>For the world,

For the world,
>In all its light & love,
And all it was meant to be,
>And damned shall be those that try to stand in our way.

Thursday, February 20, 2003

If I Had?

If I had been born,
>   When my father was,
Would I have done,
>   What he did?

Would I have pretended?
>   Married,
>>   Had a child,
>>>   And stayed hid?

Is it a choice,
>   If you do not know,
What the choices are?

If he could have been,
>   More honest, more free.
What would have happened,
>   Had he been more like me?

What would he gain,
>   What would he lose,
Perhaps less time suffering,
>   Hiding in pain and booze.

But if he had been more honest,
>   More free
Less bound by what was right,
>   What would have become of me?

Perhaps he made the right choices after all
>   Choices if I had made, instead of freedom and fun,
Would have had this poem being written in the distance future,
>   By my now never to be born son.

18 October 2006

Once More

Time has passed,
        Yet with you holding me,
No time has passed,
        For within this moment we are together.

Telling me you must go,
        You do not let go.
Knowing you must leave,
        I do not move.

You do not come back,
        But you keep telling me,
That you will be back,
        At least one more time.

Watching you as you leave,
        It does not hurt- yet,
As I know you will be back,
        At least one more time.

1982

Vampire

You came in the night,
      Gone by dawn,
Leaving your wounds
      With "I love you."

Were they said in but an act of passion?
      Shall I ever know?
Will you return tomorrow
      Or seek fresh blood?

Aids Scare

Building within me,
    Is that which was meant
To continue life,
    Not take it.

That which sustains me,
    And I cannot live without,
I cannot live with it,
    For it kills me.

From within,
    It strips me,
Of all my armor,
    Allowing me to be vulnerable,
To all on comers- defenselessly.

From its seed,
    I was conceived,
Through the passing of its seed,
    I destroy.

Within my blood,
    I have converted life,
To death,
    Yours and mine.

In Being

In being your love,
>Sometimes I must be father and mother.
Big brother and best friend,
>And sometimes not.

I give to you all I have to give,
>And when you need it, more.
And then also I take,
>And also take, more.

I have to know when to let you run away,
>So you may comeback more in touch with you,
And when to follow,
>So that you may come back more in touch with me.

I have to realize sometimes we grow better,
>Together, when we are apart,
And yet still keep in touch enough,
>So that we do not grow apart together.

One Last Time

Is it so wrong,
        For me,
To want to make love to you,
        On last time before you go.

And if I cry,
        Just hold me one last time,
So I can wipe away the tears,
        And start again.

And though you may not want to hear it,
        Can I tell you I love you,
One last time before you leave,
        So I know you know,
Just in case I never get to tell you again.

Voyeur

Side swept by sights,
    Catching corners of conversations,
Unintentionally yet eagerly eavesdropping,
    A virtuous yet vicarious voyeur.

Lustfully, lingering looks,
    Being balefully bad,
Yet dourly denying defined "dysfunction"
    When actually just,
Nurturing naturally nefarious natures.

But only when seeing it from:

Society's stuffy and stalwart standards,
    Who impose images of iron-willed icons,
As desirable deities
    Instead of insightfully seeing

Through their
    Ridiculous roles and horrendous hypocrisies
And pretentious pompous personages
    They pretend to be.

Anybody got a needle?

Alone

I find myself alone,
        Again,
Alone with no one
        to be intimate with.

I miss-
        the touch.
I miss-
        the look.

But then I remember the times,
        I hated the touch,
I was angered,
        by the look.

Am I afraid of the loneliness,
        For I am conditioned to be?
For I like to be alone and more often than not,
        Wished to be without than wish to be with.

Am I brain washed by the pitying looks,
        The vague remarks,
"Such a nice person, now if I could just
        find someone."

But I have,
        I have found me.
And I am happy to share that with
        Someone who would like to share themselves with me.

Someone,
        However,
That wants to share, without wanting to change me,
        I will do enough changing on my own.

But the world tells me I must be lonely,
        Because I am alone,

And when I tell them I am happy,
> They tell me I am brave.

I welcome someone into my life,
> With whom I would like to share with,

But not someone just so I will not be alone,
> I prefer being brave.

1994

In Need

Sometimes I just need your body,
        To be lying there,
Next to mine,
        To reach out and feel you there.

There is a certain security,
        A type of fulfillment,
So much more than physical,
        To feel your skin next to, mine.

To hold
        And to be held,
Just you and I,
        It is just,

This need I have.

Peaches

Peaches
      I watch as you
Eat peaches

I see the glistening
      Juicy lips
Wrap around that peach
      As it has wrapped around me

Dribbling juices flowing down your
      Heaving chest
Adding to the other juices that run from you

I slip and slide
      My fingertips
Down and in
      In and out
All of you

Your toes curl
      Nails scratching
Blood flows
      Drowning us in the waves
Of the breaking storms

Clutching your body
      You are my life preserver
Heaving tides
      On the tossing seas
Of life.

2005

When Friends Become Lovers

When friends become lovers,
    The world is a safer place.
And though the physical does not exist,
    Neither does the risk.

When we run from chances,
    Or only enter into them well supported,
And with half a heart, it is a sign,
    Your friends have become your lovers.

When they seem to be,
    The only ones who understand,
The only ones who know and care,
    Your friends have become your lovers.

And though your friends,
    Have their lovers,
As you have yours,
    With whom is it you share your soul?

It is in this topsy-turvy world,
    Where relationships are fleeting,
And friendships last forever,
    In which your friends are your lovers.

Whether you (or they),
    Are straight (or gay),
Male (or female),
    Are the bonds that tie you not physically,
But more than physically?

We have people:
    -too tired to fight,
    -too tired to keep trying,
    -for it is too easy,
When friends become your lover.
1982

And the Pedestal Cracks

Please, look at me again,
        See me for all my humanness,
Take me off the pedestal,
        On which you have placed me.

Sooner or later,
        You will see my frailties,
Your illusions will be shattered,
        And the pedestal cracks.

The higher you have me,
        The longer the fall,
The more likely the relationship,
        Will not survive, the fall.

And all the good that was,
        (And could have been)
Will be gone.
        And the pedestal cracks.

1982

Just Friends

Loving you as a friend,
        Was not enough for you,
You wanted more,
        More than I could give.

You, in love
        Wanted me, in love.
You did not understand
        I was, but not with you.

Feeling as if being there,
        I would turn to you,
And I did, as a friend,
        But not as the lover you wanted.

Now, you demand of me,
        What one would of a lover,
Unfortunately, not only do I not see you as a lover,
        I am beginning to not even see you as a friend.

Before I lose you as a friend,
        And any love I have for you,
Leave me now,
        So you may come back and be welcome.

Rainbows & Tears

I have chosen to remember only the rainbows
        Of our love
And of my life.

As I have chosen to forget
        That the most beautiful of the rainbow colors
Were seen because of the tears in my eyes.

And when I think of you
        And my life,
I must remember there would have been no rainbows
        If the sunshine could not have prismed through the tears.

So when you think of me,
        Remember but the colors I have given you.
For I know you have brought to me
        Some of the most beautiful colors I shall ever see.

1981

Why You Run

Age has turned you so inward,
    You are so fearful of losing,
What little happiness you still have,
    I can only feel pity for you.

You have shut out,
    Those who care,
Are you so afraid,
    They will see your happiness is an illusion

Those who have happiness,
    Usually share it,
With those they love,
    Unless their insecurities prevent this,

Is that why you run?

And the Season Turns

Mother nature's work-all but done.
        It's as brilliant and vibrant as it ever was.
This year, perhaps, even better,
        Her patchwork quilt,
Tucking in the mountains, for their winter nap.

The air, crisp & clear,
        Turns to smoke signals as I speak,
Even as I breathe.
        Her quilt, almost done,
Mother Nature prepares to rest.

There's talk of goblins in the air,
        Here tell their everywhere.
I know soon they'll be here and gone,
        And Mother Nature will go away,
Upon their coattails.

And the season turns.

1986

Looking for Rainbows

I can be as happy as the bluebird
      Who flies on fragile wings
Trying to catch a rainbow
      As he melancholically sings.

But the bluebird never tires
      In trying to find the rainbows that he seeks.
Unlike myself, who gets caught in the muck and mire,
      Stuck in a world with no mystique.

Perhaps I can learn from the bluebird
      Who drinks the sunshine and feeds upon the air.
Finding tranquility, as he does, in the being.
      Getting strength from living without care.

1979

www.ingramcontent.com/pod-product-compliance
Lightning Source LLC
LaVergne TN
LVHW020939090426
835512LV00020B/3429